WHAT YOU NEED TO KNOW
BEFORE HIRING A LAWYER

AND

WHAT YOU NEED TO KNOW
BEFORE FILING AN APPEAL

The Road Map to
The Judicial Process

Darrell A. Siggers

Disclaimer

This publication was written as a foundation to educate citizens on what they should know before hiring a lawyer and before filing an appeal. It is only to provide a basic understanding of the principles that should be employed to assure best practices between you and your lawyer and the judicial process for the benefit of all parties concerned. Do not rely solely on what is written in this book. It is only meant as a guide. You should research and determine what is the best way forward for you.

Acknowledgments

This Handbook is dedicated to the many great men and women who helped me learn the law, win my freedom, and stay strong along the hard and painful journey. Some of them include University of Michigan Professor, Paul Reingold and former Detroit Free Press writer, Jeff Gerritt, who were there in the trenches with me from the beginning to the end and remain my friends today. Director of National Capital Crime Assistance Network, Claudia Whitman, who helped me at critical moments. Attorneys Michael Waldo, Craig Daly, Wolfgang Mueller, Todd Perkins, and Laura K. Sutton, who formed the ultimate dream team for justice. And last but not least, Mary Hennig, Dr. Richard Peters, and his lovely wife Nancy, who's assistance was invaluable in proving my innocence. Each of you became and remain the best friends I've ever had. I love you all. Thanks for being the warriors for justice that you are

"Having went through 34 years of Hell in a Cell, I owe this truth to you" – Darrell Siggers

"If there is no struggle, there is no progress. Those who profess to favor freedom, and yet depreciate agitation, are men who want crops without plowing up the ground. They want rain without thunder and lightning. They want the ocean without the awful roar of its many waters. This struggle may be a moral one; or it may be a physical one; or it may be both moral and physical; but it must be a struggle. Power concedes nothing without a demand. It never did and it never will."

- Frederick Douglass

"Injustice anywhere is a threat to justice everywhere. We are caught in an inescapable network of mutuality, tied in a single garment of destiny. Whatever affects one directly, affects all indirectly."

- Martin Luther King Jr.

Introduction

My name is Darrell Siggers and I am writing this book to teach you what every person should know before hiring a lawyer and filing an appeal in court. This is something I know about all too well because I served 34 years in prison for a murder I did not commit. The charges were dismissed in 2018 and I was subsequently exonerated of all charges and released. Over my period of incarceration, I had 16 lawyers at different times and filed numerous appeals in the state and federal courts. I've also been to the United States Supreme Court, so I've learned a thing or two about hiring lawyers and filing appeals. Now, I want you to know.

Like most people who find themselves needing a lawyer, whether in a civil or criminal matter, the primary challenge is knowing how to hire him or her, and how to file an appeal if you get convicted or receive an unfair decision. Whether you are in a judicial proceeding concerning a divorce, car accident, defective product, rental disagreement, or find yourself in trouble with the law, most people at some point in their lives will need the assistance of a lawyer. And as many of you know, lawyers are not cheap. They can cost thousands of dollars to hire, and without one to help you navigate the complexities of the legal system, you can find yourself lost and in deep trouble.

When I was first arrested in 1984, I had just turned 20 years old. I was scared, confused and had no knowledge of the judicial process. To make matters worse, I, nor my family, had the money to hire a lawyer to help me fight the charges so I was appointed one by the court. And like most court-appointed lawyers, he was overworked, underpaid, and without the time and resources to properly investigate my case and provide a proper defense. I was convicted of first-degree murder and sentenced to mandatory life without parole. Needless to say, I was devastated. I felt lost, confused and betrayed and didn't have a clue as to what to do.

I was then assigned another court appointed lawyer to file my appeal. We filed a motion for a new trial which the trial court denied. We filed an application for leave to appeal the trial court's denial in the Michigan

Court of Appeals; it was denied. We also filed an appeal in the Michigan Supreme Court; it was denied.

After the state courts denied my appeals the lawyer withdrew from my case and told me I was on my own. I scraped together some money from family and friends and hired my first lawyer in 1988 to file my appeal in the federal courts. I did not know anything about this lawyer but what I was told by other inmates. I was unaware of his background or how many cases he had won or lost. All I knew was that I was desperate to file an appeal to get my conviction overturned and get out of prison, so I had my family pay the money. That was not the way to do it. Let me tell you why.

The Ten Things Every Person
Should Know Before Hiring A Lawyer

First, to find a lawyer you should contact your local state bar and ask for a list of attorneys that deal with the specific issue for which you are seeking representation. Try to get the names of at least three. Write down the specific questions you want to ask the lawyers you contact so you can make sure the lawyer understands what you want and keep notes of your conversation. If you call a lawyer and he/she is not there, send him or her an email.

Second, most people who get into trouble just give lawyers thousands of dollars to represent them, even before they know whether the lawyer can do anything to help them, which is the wrong approach. If you ask a lawyer what he or she will charge to represent you, they may quote you a retainer fee in excess of 10 or 20 thousand dollars without even knowing the facts of your case. And if the lawyer decides after investigating your case that nothing can be done to help you, do you think your money will be returned? That is why the first two things you should do when seeking to hire a lawyer is: (1) ask what is his/her fee to prepare a case evaluation, and (2) how much will he/she charge to represent you after the case evaluation is complete? Whether you need an attorney to represent you at a preliminary hearing, trial or appeal, these two initial questions are critical in determining how you can move forward.

Get everything in writing

Third, a case evaluation is essentially a written summary of the facts and issues in the case that can be won and those that cannot. A case evaluation is critically important because if you are preparing to go to a hearing or trial, it will require the lawyer to review all the reports, files, transcripts and discovery materials in your case to determine the proper defense or strategy. If you are appealing a conviction or decision that you think is unfair, the case evaluation should spell out what issues can be challenged and raised on appeal and the procedure for doing so.

It should also state whether a private investigator or forensic expert will be necessary to assist with your defense and how much he/she will cost. The cost of the case evaluation should not be the same as the cost to represent you and prepare a defense for trial or file your appeal. It should be far less because it only consists of reviewing the case and providing an analysis, not representing you in a hearing, trial or appeal.

The case evaluation puts you in a better position to make an informed decision of whether to proceed with this particular lawyer and what your options are. The bottom line is, getting a case evaluation is just plain smart.

Fourth, after the case evaluation is completed and you decide to move forward with the particular lawyer, you should then obtain a retainer agreement spelling out in specific detail what the lawyer will do at each stage that may be incurred in the process of his/her representation of your case.

A retainer agreement is essentially a contract agreement that binds you and the attorney to fulfill the terms outlined in the agreement. It should explain (a) how much money you will be required to pay, (b) what the lawyer will do in exchange for the money, (c) how many steps are in the process, and (d) what the cost will be if you lose at the first step and have to go to the next step and what the lawyer will do.

Fifth, the retainer agreement should also state how long it will take to prepare your case for any up-coming hearing, trial, or appeal.

After the retainer agreement is prepared, don't be in a rush to sign it. It is best to take it home and read it very carefully.

Always keep good records

Sixth, make a copy of the retainer agreement. If there is any language or terms in it that you do not understand, ask the lawyer to explain it to you. And if you do not agree with a particular section or term in the retainer agreement, take a pen and put a line through it, and put your initials next to the line.

Seventh, don't ever be bullied into signing an agreement you don't agree with because once you sign it, you will be stuck with it. If the lawyer does not want to remove or allow you to cross out a particular section of the retainer agreement, go to another lawyer.

Be smart with your money

Eighth, don't ever pay a lawyer all their money upfront and never pay a lawyer in cash, NEVER! Always get a money order or check and photocopy it so you will have a receipt of the transaction. This is necessary so that you will have proof that you paid the lawyer if any disagreements should occur down the road.

Keep the lawyer honest

Ninth, if you are interested in hiring the lawyer make sure you arrange a face-to-face meeting at the lawyer's office. You should never hire a lawyer without first meeting him or her face-to-face. A face-to-face meeting will allow you to see the lawyer's office and give you an idea of his/her level of success. You can look at the walls for degrees, awards, photos and other things that will tell you a little about this lawyer's history. More importantly, a face-to-face meeting will allow you to ask direct questions and gauge the lawyer's knowledge and commitment, and whether he/she can do the task you are hiring them to do. It will also allow you to ask him/her for references from past clients.

The lawyer should be willing to meet with you without charging you any fee. Finally, try to also communicate with lawyers through emails/texts because it allows you to keep a record of your communications for future reference. Keep notes of dates, times and what the lawyer says whenever you talk to him/her on the phone, along with all emails and letters that you send and receive from the lawyer. This protects you and the lawyer.

Get the lawyer who will fight for you

Tenth, a lawyer's duty to the client is to uphold his/her constitutional rights and to represent you zealously. Lawyers cannot guarantee an outcome, and any lawyer who tells you he/she can is not being honest with you because that's not how the legal system works. That may work in the movies, but not in real life. What you are primarily paying a lawyer to do is to win your case if possible, but if not, to assist you in obtaining the best result, in light of the circumstances, with the understanding that there are no guarantees. Lawyers are the warriors of justice. They are officers of the court and representatives of the People! They make the legal system work by means of litigation and results.

The hope is that your lawyer, no matter what the circumstance, will be your warrior of justice. Knowing these simple rules will help you if you should ever need to hire a lawyer and what to do moving forward if you already have one.

Other things you should
do before hiring a lawyer

If you want to be really thorough you should: (a) do a name search of the lawyer on the internet, (b) find out how long the lawyer has been practicing law, and (c) contact the state bar to inquire if any complaints have been filed on the lawyer.

Please understand that this handbook cannot provide all the answers. It is only a general guide to the basics of what you need to know before hiring a lawyer. There are also ten things you should know before filing an appeal.

The Ten Things Every Person
Should Know Before Filing An Appeal

If you lose at the first step, there's usually a way to appeal and try to get the previous decision reversed or set aside.

First, you should know that there are thousands of administrative, civil and criminal appeals filed every day all over our nation, and in many jurisdictions, courts are overwhelmed by the number of these appeals. And because there are not enough clerks and judges to process these appeals in some municipalities and judicial districts, it creates a backlog, which is why appeals can take up to a few months to a few years before a decision is reached. You can always call the clerk of the court to ask questions before filing your appeal, and you should.

Be realistic about your chances

Unfortunately, filing an appeal usually means the client lost at the previous level or did not receive the result he or she thought was fair. Appeals are always hard to win because you must prove the verdict or decision you received was wrong. What this means is, without getting into a lot of legal mumbo jumbo, you have to show that the judge, jury, or decision-maker in your case: (1) failed to follow some procedural rule, (2) violated your constitutional rights in some way and/or (3) that your attorney's representation was ineffective.

The law can be complicated, but you must try to learn the parts of it that govern your situation. A lot of people are intimidated by the law and think it is too complex. However, you should think of the law as being a tool used to settle disputes. And if you are going to win, you must learn how to use this tool. You don't have to learn everything about the law, only what you need to know to protect your rights and prevent them from being denied. The ultimate goal should be to figure out how to win or settle your case with the best and fairest result possible.

Do your research

Second, after obtaining the case evaluation and retainer agreement, you should study the court rule, statute or constitutional law on which your defense or arguments on appeal are based. Go on the internet or to the library and look it up. Don't worry about not understanding all the legal terms; some lawyers don't understand them either. All you need to do is learn what law or court rule: (1)

protects your rights, (2) why it entitles you to a new hearing, new trial, or a better result, and (3) why it requires the previous decision to be reversed or vacated. The thing is, you have to be willing to study and read the law that pertains to your case over and over again until you understand it and not let it intimidate you.

Lawyers can be great advocates for us, but you cannot rely solely on your lawyer to protect your rights, because no matter what happens, it will be you who will suffer the consequences. You must learn the law for yourself, at least the parts of it that pertain to you. Also, if you hire a lawyer, it is vitally important that you let him/her know not to file any motions or appeals on your behalf without approval from you in writing.

Let's talk about the process. If you lose at a hearing or trial and want to appeal, the first thing you must do is obtain the records pertaining to the decision that you believe was unfair and should be reversed. What this means is, you must obtain a copy of the police file, prosecutor file and court file. If the hearing or trial you seek to challenge was transcribed by a stenographer, you must get a copy of the transcripts. You must also obtain any motions, responses and written opinions that you seek to challenge. Finally, you must obtain a copy of the docket journal or otherwise referred to as a register of entries. This is a list of dates, times and all activities that occurred during the proceedings. You need this document to verify: (1) the dates of the proceedings you are appealing, (2) when any motions were officially filed, (3) the dates they were decided, and (4) the names of the judges who decided them.

Without documentation, you can't fight

Third, the point is, you have to try to get a copy of all the records involved with your case because it is these records that you or your lawyer will be using to file the appeal. Without them, you cannot successfully challenge the prior decisions.

Now the appeal. In some cases, the lawyers can get the transcripts and other records to file the appeal, and if he/she does, ask him/her to make a copy for you. However, if you can obtain a copy yourself from the police, prosecutor or court, you should because you want to have copies of all records and files that pertain to you or the decision you are challenging.

Court transcripts and records from the court clerk, police or prosecutor can cost up to $2 a page; however, if you are an incarcerated inmate, the U.S. Supreme Court has stated that indigent defendants in a criminal case are entitled to one free copy of their court transcripts and other records. Griffin v. Illinois, (1956). You want to get and hang on to these documents so you can study and familiarize yourself with the legal basis of your case, which I suggest that you do.

You don't have to know the law as well as a lawyer, but you should try to learn as much as you can so you can help your lawyer help you and not depend solely on him/her.

Once you obtain the records and files, it may be a good idea to go to a photocopy center like Staples, Office Max or FedEx and have them put on a thumb drive so that if you have to take them to another lawyer, you can give him/her the paper copy and keep the thumb drive. This way you will always have an accessible copy of your records.

Learn the rules

Fourth, for citizens convicted of felony offenses, the U.S. Constitution and statutes in your state entitle you to one full appeal, which the courts have termed your "appeal of right" or "right of appeal." What this means is, a criminal defendant is entitled to file an appeal to challenge his or her conviction. Although the rules are different in most judicial jurisdictions, this is a fundamental principle in all states as determined by the U.S. Supreme Court.

In most states, after a defendant is convicted, if he or she cannot afford a lawyer, this person can request that the court appoint an appellate lawyer to represent them. As part of a defendant's appeal of right (or automatic appeal) the court usually appoints counsel to file an appeal on his/her behalf. However, in cases where the defendant pleads guilty, once a defendant enters a guilty plea, he or she waives the right to a trial by jury and thereby also waives the right to an automatic appeal. What this means is, unlike in cases where a defendant is found guilty at a trial, the appellate courts are not required to hear the appeal, making it discretionary.

Pleading Guilty

For those who have pled guilty, it is not easy to withdraw a plea or get it set aside because, by pleading guilty you waive all rights to challenge your plea. However, there are two ways you might try: (1) the judge must read almost verbatim from the court rules and ask you specific questions to assure that your waiver of the right to a trial is knowing, intelligent and understanding. If your plea was not knowing, intelligent and understanding, it is invalid and you should be able to get it vacated. If you want to know what the terms "knowing, intelligent and understanding" mean, go to your library and look them up in the Black's Law Dictionary. The Black's Law Dictionary is a legal dictionary that lawyers and judges rely on to define legal terms.

If you have already been sentenced, get the transcript of the plea hearing. Compare what the judge said to you before you entered the plea against the requirements of the court rules governing guilty pleas. If the judge did not ask you the questions set forth in the court rules, you may be able to challenge the guilty plea as being invalid, (2) the guilty plea rules require that before a judge can accept your plea, there must be a factual basis – meaning you must fully admit to the crime on the record and fulfill all the requirements for establishing guilt for the charged offense. If a factual basis was not sufficiently established in what you said when you pled guilty, your plea may be invalid and subject to challenge on appeal. The appellate lawyer has the option of filing a motion to withdraw your plea or to get it vacated in the court where the plea occurred.

If you had a sham trial with a trial lawyer you think was ineffective and did not do a good job, it may be better for the appellate lawyer to seek relief in the trial court to preserve particular issues and create a record for the appellate court to review. What this means is, if there were mistakes made by your lawyer or the trial judge that are not on the record, or reflected in the transcript of the trial, it is important to get them on the record before going to the next step.

Typically, if the error or mistake you seek to challenge is not on the record, the appellate court won't have anything to review or which to base their decision. So, filing a motion for new trial or for resentencing, allows you to put any mistakes that you think were made on the record, and if the court grants your motion or request for resentencing, you won't have to waste valuable time appealing to the appellate court.

Making the right choice

Fifth, the lawyer also has the option of filing a defendant's appeal directly to the appellate court, which in most jurisdictions, is called the court of appeals, which usually consists of a three-judge panel. Whether a defendant should file a motion for a new trial or resentencing in the trial court before going to the appeals court depends on the circumstances and facts of the case. The bottom line is, appellate courts generally will only review issues on appeal if: (1) you can establish that a constitutional violation occurred that denied you a fair trial, (2) the trial court failed to follow a particular court rule or procedure that denied you a fair trial, and (3) the issues are clear and on the record for the appellate court to review. If you decide to file an appeal in the appellate court and do not obtain relief, you can go to the Supreme Court.

There are books and procedural manuals that can explain the appellate rules, time limits and process in which to file and challenge lower court decisions which you can find in the library and on-line.

Pay attention to time limits

Sixth, it is imperative that you find out the time limits for when you have to file your appeal with the court because if you don't get your appeal filed in the time set by the court rule, you will forfeit your appeal. If you don't know how much time you have to file an appeal, you can either go to the library, look it up on your computer (or phone) or ask a lawyer. If you ask a lawyer, also ask him/her what court rule the time limit is based so you can read it and know for yourself. When the lawyer tells you what the court rule is go online or to your library and look it up. Don't ever be afraid to ask your lawyer questions. Whether you are paying a lawyer, or he/she is appointed by the court, they work for you, which means you are entitled to ask questions.

If you are going to ask a lawyer questions, remember that it is always best to write the questions down so they will be clear and you will have time to think about what you want to say or ask.

Appealing to the federal courts

If you lose in the state appellate courts, the Constitution allows a defendant to challenge his/her state court conviction or sentence in the federal court through what is referred to as a Petition for Writ of Habeas Corpus. A Petition for Writ of Habeas Corpus must be based on constitutional grounds that your confinement is an illegal restraint of your liberty – meaning your right to be free.

Court rules in all states and local districts provide men and women the right to challenge their prison confinement in the federal court beginning with the United States District Court if they lose in the state court. Court rules provide that a federal Petition for Writ of Habeas Corpus must generally be filed in the district where the crime occurred or the location where the person filing it resides.

Seventh, three of the most important things that you must know before filing a federal petition for habeas corpus are: (1) you must be in custody and have followed all the steps and time limits in the state appellate courts – meaning you timely filed your appeal in the appeals court and supreme court of your state, or you will be barred, (2) you only have one year to get it filed after you receive a decision from the highest state court on your appeal of right, usually the supreme court in your state, and (3) the issues you are seeking to appeal must have been argued and presented in the state courts from a constitutional standpoint – meaning you must have cited in your state court appellate application/brief some provision of the constitution or a U.S. Supreme Court decision.

I realize this might seem complex or even confusing, but if you do not complete these steps, your case will likely be dismissed on procedural grounds and may never be heard by the judge. If you decide to file a Petition for Writ of Habeas Corpus, you can write to the U.S. District Court clerk and obtain copies of the required habeas corpus forms necessary to file your petition. The forms are free and contain instructions as to how to complete them.

Know your options

Alternatively, if you decide you do not want to file a Petition for Habeas Corpus, you could file a Petition for Writ of Certiorari directly to the U.S. Supreme Court which will provide you an additional 90 days, plus the one year, to get it filed. A Petition for Writ of Certiorari is a legal pleading that provides the U.S. Supreme Court the authority to review your petition and grant you a new trial, resentencing or any relief it chooses. The U.S. Supreme Court, with its nine justices, is the highest court in the land. And although they receive appeals from all 50 states, they rarely ever grant relief, and when they do decide cases, their opinions generally affect all states and provide mandates for which all courts are bound to follow.

If you decide not to file for Certiorari and want to preserve your right to file a Petition for Writ of Habeas Corpus, you must properly file a post-conviction motion to stop the 1-year time limit from running out on you. This is because, as I said above, you only have one year to file your Petition for Writ of Habeas Corpus after you receive a decision from the highest state court. What this means is, if you properly file a post-conviction motion for a new trial or for resentencing, it temporarily stops the 1-year clock from running.

The one-year time limit is referred to as the 1-year Statute of Limitations. The way to stop the 1-year clock from running is by filing a post-conviction motion or application challenging your conviction or sentence, usually in the circuit or district court where you were convicted. Second appeals and post-conviction motions are discretionary, meaning a court is not required to hear them as they would your first (automatic) appeal of right.

If your post-conviction motion is denied and you timely appeal to the court of appeals and state supreme court, the 1-year clock does not begin to run again until you receive a decision from the state supreme court. What this means is, the clock is stayed (stopped) so any days in between filing your appeal from the trial court to the court of appeals and from the court of appeals to the supreme court, don't count against you as long as your appeals are properly filed and timely.

Follow the court rules

Eighth, if you fail to comply with any of the time periods, the clock starts to run again on the last day you had to appeal to the next step, and you will be procedurally barred from filing a Petition for Writ of Habeas Corpus. If, however, you do meet all the state court appellate time limits, once you receive a decision from the highest state court – meaning the state supreme court - the clock begins to run again. So, for example, if it took you 6 months to get your post-conviction motion/application filed after the state supreme court denied your appeal of right, you will only have 6 months left from the date the supreme court denied your post-conviction appeal.

I know all of this can seem confusing, which is why you should re-read this section until it sinks in. You should also read the Federal Rules of Appellate Procedure to fully understand the time limits that govern your case. You can find these rules in the library or on-line under 28 U.S.C. §2254 (for prisoners confined in state custody) and 28 U.S.C. §2255 (for prisoners confined in federal custody). You can also type in these keywords on your computer or phone, "How to file a petition for writ of habeas corpus" and find the answers you need.

Each federal district court has its own local rules that govern its practices and procedures. You must read them to make sure you are correctly following all the rules. Usually, you can simply write to the clerk of the district court where you intend to file your habeas petition to get the local rules or go online. You should also check out the Federal Rules of Civil Procedure and Federal Rules of Appellate Procedure.

What judges look for

A Petition for Writ of Habeas Corpus can be a powerful tool to seek justice in the federal court from an illegal conviction and is generally decided by one judge. When deciding habeas petitions, the judge can grant a Petition for Writ of Habeas Corpus if the state courts made a decision denying your appeal that was: (1) an unreasonable application of the facts, (2) violated the Constitution, and/or (3) was contrary to a decision by the United States Supreme Court.

Just ask the computer

If the U.S. District Court denies your Petition for Writ of Habeas Corpus, you can file a Motion for Certificate of Appealability to the U.S. Court of Appeals for your jurisdiction. If you do not know how to file a Motion for a Certificate of Appealability you can enter the key phrase on your computer or phone, "how to file a certificate of appealability" and learn what you need to do and how to do it. You can also go to www.uscourts.gov. There is a lot of "how-to" information in your library and on your computer.

The process

Ninth, in most states like Michigan, there are three judicial levels: the trial court, (with individual judges) Michigan Appeals Court (with three-judge panels) and Michigan Supreme Court (with seven judges). It is the same on the federal level where there is the U.S. District Court, (with individual judges) U.S. Court of Appeals (with three-judge panels) and the U.S. Supreme Court (with nine judges, or justices as they are sometimes called).

If the offense you were tried and convicted of occurred in the State court, you can utilize appellate procedures to appeal your case to the federal court system. But you should know, in most States, the higher you go in the court system, the harder it can be to win your appeal because judges don't like reversing the decisions of other judges unless you have clear evidence that a constitutional violation has occurred that denied you a fair trial, or evidence that establishes your innocence.

Innocence means innocent

Judges have the discretion to grant relief in almost any case if you can establish that a miscarriage of justice has occurred. A miscarriage of justice was defined by the U.S. Supreme Court to mean that a constitutional error has occurred that has probably caused the conviction of an innocent man or woman. Schlup v. Delo (1995). What this means is, that you were denied a fair trial by a violation of your constitutional rights and that had the constitutional error not occurred, you would have likely been found not guilty. However, keep in mind that if you are claiming innocence, you have to show that: (1) it was not you who committed the crime, (2) that you had nothing to do with it, and (3) that you have been misidentified in some way.

Some inmates believe that if they can prove that they should have been convicted of a lesser offense, they can meet the standard of innocence. However, this is legal innocence or otherwise termed "insufficiency of evidence," which is different than actual innocence as defined above.

What to expect

If you have filed your first appeal and been denied, many inmates find themselves in the position of having to file post-conviction motions or second appeals because their lawyers failed to raise certain issues or based on new evidence that they have discovered after their conviction.

If you are raising an appeal based on an issue that your lawyer failed to raise you will essentially have to show that, had the lawyer raised the issue, the result of the proceeding would have been different – meaning you would have been found not guilty or received a lesser sentence. If you are raising a claim of newly discovered evidence, you will have to show that the evidence is actually new and not merely newly available. There is a difference. You must also show that the new evidence could not have been discovered previously through the exercise of due diligence – meaning it was not likely that you could have found this evidence earlier. And finally, you must also show that the evidence would have likely changed the result of the proceeding.

You should, however, know that our judicial system is not designed to grant new trials or vacate convictions and sentences. 95% of all appeals at all levels are denied no matter what constitutional violation occurred during the trial or how unfair your trial was.

When courts review your post-conviction motion and/or appeal, they are looking for: (1) how were you denied a fair trial, (2) what constitutional violations occurred, and (3) whether there was still enough evidence to convict you despite the unfairness of your trial. The Sixth and Fourteenth Amendments to the United States Constitution guarantee every citizen a fair trial.

However, even where you can show a clear constitutional violation, courts don't have to grant you relief. They can simply say that the constitutional error was harmless. What this means is, although you may be able to show a constitutional violation, if it appears to the court that there is overwhelming evidence you committed the crime, they will most likely deny relief. They do so on the basis that even if the constitutional error had not occurred, you still would have been found guilty in light of all the evidence as a whole. So, you must show that, had the constitutional error not occurred, the jury would have found you not guilty.

If you have new and reliable evidence that you believe proves your innocence, it may be best to first submit your case to an Innocence Project or Conviction Integrity Unit (CIU). If an Innocence Project or CIU accepts your case, you have a far better chance of obtaining relief than if you proceed pro se. Innocence Projects generally have good resources, smart investigative techniques and skilled teams of lawyers to help establish and submit your claim to the court. Conviction Integrity Units have the same but are under the commission of the county prosecutors (or district attorneys) office.

The difference is, unlike courts that are limited by procedural court rules, Conviction Integrity Units are not. The Conviction Integrity Units' primary goal is to search for the truth and determine if you are innocent and/or wrongfully convicted.

Always use best practices

Tenth, even if you learn all these things, I am not saying you should try to represent yourself because it is always best to have a lawyer representing you. You just have to do all you can, by following the above steps, to make sure he or she is the right lawyer for you. That is why you must get a retainer agreement that spells out all the terms of what the lawyer will do, and what steps he/she will take to do it.

The retainer agreement should also include what the lawyer will charge to read all the records in the case and prepare a case evaluation. Remember, the case evaluation requires that the lawyer explain to you in writing, after reading all the relevant records involved, the strengths and weaknesses of your case. The case evaluation should summarize the facts and legal issues involved and what can be done to challenge an illegal arrest or unlawful conviction. If your legal matter is important to you, using these tools and learning the rules that govern it will provide you with the information you need to make the best choices and obtain the best results for you.

Make all parties accountable

This handbook is only a guide to teach you the general principles of what you should know before hiring a lawyer and filing an appeal. If you use these simple rules and tools, it will be hard for any lawyer to trick you or pull the wool over your eyes. These tools protect the client and the lawyer because they make both parties accountable.

Other things you should
know before filing an appeal

Although I am trying to make this handbook simple without a lot of complicated legal jargon that no one understands but lawyers, if you are challenging an illegal arrest or unlawful conviction, there are certain guaranteed constitutional rights that every citizen should know. I will list a few of them that I think are amongst the most important: (1) the right to remain silent, (2) the right to see all the evidence the police and prosecutor have against you, (3) the right to notice of the charges in person, (4) the right to a fair trial and an impartial jury; and (5) the right to have an effective attorney represent you during the pretrial proceedings, at trial and on your appeal of right.

Right to silence

Let me explain these constitutional rights to you one at a time, starting first with your right to remain silent. The right to silence is a legal principle that guarantees any individual the right to refuse to answer questions from law enforcement officers or court officials.

The right covers a number of issues centered on the right of the accused or the defendant to refuse to comment or provide an answer when questioned, either before or during legal proceedings in a court of law. This can be the right to avoid self-incrimination or the right to remain silent when questioned. The right may include the provision that adverse inferences cannot be made by the judge or jury regarding the refusal by a defendant to answer questions before or during a trial, hearing or any other legal proceeding. This right constitutes only a small part of the defendant's rights as a whole.

In the United States, informing suspects of their right to remain silent and of the consequences for giving up that right forms a key part of the Miranda warning. What this means is, if you are ever arrested or detained by any law enforcement officer, you don't have to answer any questions this person asks you. You have the absolute right to remain silent. If you give up that right, anything you say can and will be used against you.

Law enforcement officials can lie to suspects to get them to make statements. They can falsely accuse suspects of committing crimes. They can make fake promises to get suspects to confess. They can use all kinds of tricks, and in many cases, they do, to get suspects to confess to crimes they didn't commit or make incriminating statements.

The right to remain silent remains throughout the entire proceeding – meaning you do not have to answer any questions from anyone, including a judge or prosecutor. If asked a question, you can simply say, "I invoke my Fifth Amendment right to remain silent." So, if you are arrested or detained, your best bet is to remain silent and ask for a lawyer. Once you make a statement you are usually stuck with it, so keep your mouth shut!

The U.S. Supreme Court has held that once you ask for a lawyer, law enforcement officials must stop all questioning, so always ask for a lawyer if you are arrested.

The right to Brady evidence

The Brady doctrine is a great pretrial discovery rule that was established by the United States Supreme Court in Brady v.

Maryland (1963). The rule requires that the prosecution must turn over all exculpatory evidence to the defendant in a criminal case. In Kyles v. Whitley, (1995), the U.S. Supreme Court held that the police are part of the prosecution's team; therefore, it doesn't matter if it is the police who withhold the exculpatory evidence, the withholding is imputed to the prosecutor. Exculpatory evidence is favorable evidence tending to exonerate the defendant. The Supreme Court concluded in Kyles, that the suppression by the prosecution of evidence favorable to an accused violates due process where the evidence is material either to guilt or to punishment, irrespective of the good faith or bad faith of the prosecution.

Legal standard

In Kyles v. Whitley, the Supreme Court reaffirmed Brady v. Maryland (1963), and stated the question is not whether the defendant would more likely than not have received a different verdict with the evidence, but whether in its absence he received a fair trial, understood as a trial resulting in a verdict worthy of confidence.

The point is, if you have been arrested, always ask the prosecutor and/or make a motion to the court for your discovery materials. Discovery materials usually consist of the warrant and complaint filed against you, any police reports, lab reports and all other evidence the prosecution intends to use against you. You must know what the prosecution plans to use against you so you can defend against it.

The Sixth Amendment

The Sixth Amendment grants criminal defendants the right to a speedy and public trial by an impartial jury consisting of jurors from the state and district in which the crime was alleged to have been committed. Under the impartial jury requirement, jurors must be unbiased, and the jury must consist of a representative cross-section of the community.

The right to a jury only applies to offenses in which the penalty is imprisonment for longer than six months. The Supreme Court has held that the requirement of a public trial is not absolute and that both the government and the defendant can in some cases request a closed trial. The Sixth Amendment requires that criminal defendants be given notice of the nature and cause of accusations against them.

The amendment's Confrontation Clause gives criminal defendants the right to confront and cross-examine witnesses, while the Compulsory Process Clause provides criminal defendants the right to call their own witnesses and, in some cases, compel witnesses to testify.

The Assistance of Counsel Clause grants criminal defendants the right to be assisted by counsel. In Gideon v. Wainwright (1966) and subsequent cases, the Supreme Court held that a public defender must be provided to criminal defendants unable to afford an attorney in all trials where the defendant faces the possibility of imprisonment. This is to say, the Sixth Amendment grants us multiple rights.

Did your lawyer properly represent you

In the United States ineffective assistance of counsel is a claim raised by a convicted criminal defendant on the basis that his or her lawyer performed so ineffectively (badly) that it deprived him or her the guaranteed right by the Assistance of Counsel Clause of the Sixth Amendment to the United States Constitution. Having the benefit of counsel or assistance of counsel means that you have a competent attorney representing you. Competence is defined as reasonable professional assistance and is defined in part by prevailing professional norms and standards. To prove you received ineffective assistance, a criminal defendant must show two things: (1) deficient performance by counsel, and (2) resulting prejudice, in that, but for the deficient performance, the result of the proceeding would have been different. Strickland v Washington (1984).

Put yourself in the position to win

Put yourself in the best position to win by adding a private investigator and/or forensic expert to your team. If you are seeking to prevail on a civil or criminal claim, having an independent expert to support your case puts you in a better position to win. This is true also if you are filing a post-conviction motion for a new trial or resentencing.

There are all kinds of experts; crime reconstruction experts, firearm experts, DNA experts, eyewitness experts, voice recognition experts and many others. You just have to find the right one for you. Having an expert to write a report in support of your defense puts you in a better position to win because with an expert, you have scientific proof of your claim, and not just a bald assertion.

Also, if your case is based on a new witness or a recanting witness, private investigators can make a big difference, especially if they make a video of the witness's statement and provide an affidavit. If you get a video of the witness's statement and they later choose not to testify on your behalf, you can present the video to the court. If you are going to hire a forensic expert or private investigator, do your due diligence and make sure their credentials are on point for what you need to prove your case. This is the era of CSI and judges tend to listen to experts and private investigators more so than defendants.

Conclusion

I could go on and on with what you should know before hiring a lawyer and what you should know before filing an appeal. However, the purpose of this handbook is not to bore you with a lot of legal jargon, rather to provide the basic rules and tools necessary to equip anyone who seeks the knowledge to use it.

Having spent 34 years incarcerated for a crime I did not commit, is an experience that no citizen should have to suffer. In 1984, at 20 years old, I was a layman and didn't know anything about the law. My unjust first-degree murder conviction was the most painful experience of my life.

Knowing that I was innocent made it even worse. I had 16 lawyers over my period of incarceration and filed numerous appeals. The valuable lessons I learned provides me the unique experience and insight to teach you what you should know before hiring a lawyer and filing an appeal. Had I known what I am telling you in this handbook, I would have saved thousands of dollars on lawyers and probably not went to prison. Every day that I could go to the law library for the 34 years I was unjustly incarcerated, I did, and I learned everything I could about the law. With this knowledge and the blessings of God, I was exonerated on October 19, 2018.

My advice to you is to learn all you can about the law and reach out to every legal organization you can for help and never stop fighting. I didn't and now I'm free. It was not easy, but I never gave up, because I was not going to surrender my life to an unjust conviction, nor should you.

Since being exonerated, I created ACCESS PLUS to provide assistance to our communities and the men and women incarcerated who need help. For more information about the programs of ACCESS PLUS please visit our website, www.legalaccessplus.com.

Don't be a sucker! Know your legal rights.

GLOSSARY

Acquittal: A release or discharge from a charge.

Adjudication: A court's judgment in a case. Issues once raised on appeal, once ruled on by a court are then considered adjudicated.

Affirm: To confirm or agree with a lower court's rulings or decisions by a higher court.

Aggravating Circumstances: Actions committed or circumstances surrounding the commission of a crime which increases its seriousness.

Appeal: Petitioning of a higher court to correct errors made by the lower court.

Appellant: The person or party seeking an appeal.

Appellate Court: A higher court which has jurisdiction to hear appeals and review the decisions of lower courts. Also called the Appeals Court.

Appellee: The person or party against whom an appeal is taken. Also known as the respondent.

Arraignment: Procedure by which a defendant is called before a court to be notified of the charges against him/her and to be asked how he/she pleads to those charges.

Bail: Release of a defendant from custody on his/her own assurance, or that of another person (bail bondsman) that the defendant will appear in court at the appointed times to face the charges pending before the court. As a practical matter, bail is rarely ever granted in first-degree murder cases.

Bill of Indictment: Written accusation presented to a Grand Jury with the claims the State wishes to prove against a defendant, upon which the Grand Jury may return a "True Bill".

Bill of Information: Written accusation presented to a Trial Court alleging crimes committed, to bring a defendant into the Court's jurisdiction for trial.

Bill of Particulars: Detailed statement of charges or other information by one party to notify an opposing party of all the information of which it should be aware. Commonly included as a Motion for Discovery, Inspection, and Bill of Particulars.

Challenge for Cause: Removing, or striking of a potential juror by the Court at the request of either the State or the Defense, or on the court's own initiative, for the potential juror's inability to be fair or a stated inability to impose the death penalty; not to be confused with a peremptory challenge.

Circuit Court of Appeals: Intermediate appeals court (CCA) between the trial court level and the State Supreme Court, with the power to hear appeals, usually during habeas corpus (post-conviction) proceedings. Thirty-eight States operate a Circuit Court of Appeals.

Cross-examination: Questioning of a witness by an opposing party after direct examination.

Death Qualification: Qualifying of jurors during jury selection to ensure that each person could impose a death sentence where the charges and circumstances may warrant it.

Defendant: Individuals against whom charges or accusations are made.

Direct Appeal: First appeal following conviction in the trial court to the State's highest court responsible for reviewing all convictions and sentences of death. Mandatory appeal.

Direct Evidence: Evidence from witnesses who testify concerning their actual knowledge of facts concerning a case.

Direct Examination: First questioning of a witness by the party who called him/her to testify.

District Attorney: Attorney either appointed or elected to represent the State or federal government in a specified district.

Documentary Evidence: Evidence which is written or from documents.

Exculpatory: Clearing from fault or guilt.

Exhibit: Any paper, document or other physical item introduced as evidence.

Felony: Crime of a more serious nature than a misdemeanor, punishable by imprisonment or death as determined by State or Federal laws.

Foreman/person: Member of a jury appointed to preside over the jury.

Grand Jury: Body of people appointed to hear accusations of crimes, a Bill of Indictment filed by the State, to determine if sufficient probable cause exists for the accused to be prosecuted. The Grand Jury may issue an indictment, a "True Bill" or refuse to indict.

Habeas Corpus: Latin: "you have the body". A Writ requiring a person to be brought before a court or judge, whether physically or by appeal brief, to determine if that person has been detained or imprisoned wrongfully. Such writs are directed towards the official who has custody of the defendant. A habeas corpus appeal is frequently referred to as a Post-Conviction appeal.

Hearing: Formal or informal proceeding or examination in court.

Jurisdiction: Authority of a court to hear a case or appeal and enforce judgment.

Impeachment Evidence: Evidence or testimony a party may use to challenge and discredit an opposing party's witness, such as previously contradictory statements made by the witness.

Indictment: Written accusation, or "true bill", from a Grand Jury against a person accused of committing a crime, allowing further prosecution.

Indirect Evidence: Circumstantial evidence.

Jury: Group of people selected from the community to hear testimony and evidence in a trial and determine the guilt or innocence of the accused. In capital cases, the jury also determines the sentence to be imposed.

Jury Instructions: Directions given to a jury by the judge before it begins deliberation in a trial as to the law concerning how and for what the jury may find a defendant guilty or not guilty. In capital cases, what sentences it may impose.

Legislation: The act of making or enacting laws, or a law or the body of laws already enacted.

Legislature: State body of elected officials with the power to make, amend, or repeal laws.

Misdemeanor: A crime or offense of a nature less serious than a felony as determined by State or Federal law.

Mistrial: Termination of a trial due to some error in the proceedings, or the jury's inability to reach a verdict during deliberations.

Mitigating Circumstances: Circumstances of a crime or of the defendant which tend to lessen the punishment due to the crime.

Motion: Verbal or written request by a party made to the court for a ruling or order on its behalf.

Motion for Discovery: Motion to cause an adversary to produce evidence or information to which the party is entitled by law, commonly called a "motion for discovery, inspection, and Bill of Particulars", usually filed in the pre-trial phase.

Opinion: Written reason given by a judge for his/her ruling.

Oral Evidence: Evidence which is spoken; direct evidence.

Peremptory Challenge: Challenge or strike, allotted to both State and Defense, the number of which varies from State to State, during Jury selection. It allows both sides to exclude prospective jurors from sitting on the jury without giving reasons.

Post-Conviction Appeal: Appeal process following the direct appeal, also known as habeas corpus, first at the State level, then at the federal level (Federal habeas corpus).

Precedent: previous legal decision, ruling or opinion which serves as a guide for similar cases that follow.

Pro Se: On your own behalf; filing your own briefs.

Probable Cause: Sufficient initial evidence for the belief that an individual has committed a crime.

Rebuttal: Re-examination or questioning of a witness after an opposing party has cross-examined him/her. The second argument allowing the State in opening and closing arguments to a jury after the Defense has presented its argument.

Rebuttal Evidence: Evidence which either explains or discredits evidence presented by an opposing party.

State's Evidence: Testimony of an accomplice to a crime given on behalf of the State against other participants in the crime, in return for a deal or special treatment.

Statute: Law enacted by a State's legislature or the Federal government.

Stipulation: Matter agreed upon between two parties, the State and Defense, usually to save time.

Subpoena: Writ issued by a court causing a person to appear before it.

Supreme Court: The highest court in a State; the State's court of last resort. The United States Supreme Court, the highest court in the country.

Testify: Give evidence as a witness.

Transcript: Written copy of any document. Complete written records of a trial.

True Bill: Indictment issued by a Grand Jury from a Bill of Indictment, submitted to it by the State indicating it has found probable cause for a defendant to be tried for the crime alleged against him/her.

U.S. Court of Appeals: Federal Circuit Court of Appeals. There are 11 U.S. Courts of Appeal, plus one for Washington, D.C., each with jurisdiction over a certain area of the U.S., for the purpose of hearing appeals from the States within their jurisdiction.

Voir Dire: Process of Jury Selection.

Warrant: 1). Writ issued by a court ordering the arrest of a person. 2). Writ issued by a court allowing officers to search private property.

Writ: Order issued by a court directing an officer, official, or lower court to do or refrain from doing something in compliance with its direction.

Writ of Certiorari (writ of cert): Writ directing a lower court to provide a record of proceedings for review to a higher court. The essence of a writ of cert is usually an appellant appealing to the U.S. Supreme Court for a new trial or resentencing.